Keeping Unusual Pets

Lizards

Peter Heathcote

Chicago, Illinois

www.heinemannraintree.com
Visit our website to find out
more information about
Heinemann-Raintree books.

To order:
☎ Phone 888-454-2279
🖳 Visit www.heinemannraintree.com
to browse our catalog and order online.

© 2002, 2010 Heinemann Library
an imprint of Capstone Global Library, LLC
Chicago, Illinois

Edited by Louise Galpine, Megan Cotugno, and Laura Knowles
Designed by Kim Miracle and Ryan Frieson
Picture research by Mica Brancic
Originated by Capstone Global Library Ltd 2010
Printed and bound in China by Leo Paper Products Ltd

14 13 12 11 10
10 9 8 7 6 5 4 3 2 1

Library of Congress Cataloging-in-Publication Data
Heathcote, Peter.
 Lizards / Peter Heathcote. -- 2nd ed.
  p. cm. -- (Keeping unusual pets)
 Includes bibliographical references and index.
 ISBN 978-1-4329-3853-6 (hc)
 1. Lizards as pets--Juvenile literature. I. Title.
 SF459.L5H43 2010
 639.3'95--dc22
                    2009035538

Acknowledgments
The author and publisher are grateful to the following for permission to reproduce copyright material: Bruce Coleman p. **6 top** (Animal Ark); © Capstone Global Library Ltd pp. **6 bottom, 7, 8, 9 top, 10, 14, 15, 16, 17 top, 17 bottom, 18 top, 18 bottom, 21 bottom, 24, 27, 28 top, 29 bottom, 30, 32, 33 top, 33 bottom, 34, 35 top, 38 top, 41 top, 42, 43 top, 43 bottom, 44, 45 top** (Tudor Photography), **45 bottom** (Maria Joannou); © Capstone Publishers pp. **12, 13, 20, 21 top, 23 top, 23 bottom, 25, 26, 28 bottom, 31 top, 31 bottom** (Karon Dubke); FLPA p. **11 top** (Silvestris Fotoservice); iStockphoto p. **22** (© Petr Koudelka); NHPA pp. **4, 41 bottom** (Daniel Heuclin), **9 bottom, 35 bottom**; OSF pp. **5** (www.photolibrary.com/David Fox) **11 bottom** (www.photolibrary. com/BrianKenney); RSPCA pp. **19** (Ken King), **37 top, 37 bottom, 39** (Stephen J Divers); Science Photo Library pp. **36** (CNRI), **38 bottom** (Sinclair Stammers), 40 top (David Scharf).

Cover photograph of a bearded dragon lizard reproduced with permission of iStock (© Andrey Parfenov).

We would like to thank Judy Tuma and Rob Lee for their invaluable help in the preparation of this book.

Every effort has been made to contact copyright holders of material reproduced in this book. Any omissions will be rectified in subsequent printings if notice is given to the publisher.

Contents

Any words appearing in the text in bold, **like this**, are explained in the glossary.

What Is a Lizard?

Lizards are one of the oldest groups of animals alive today. Their ancestors lived alongside the dinosaurs during the **Cretaceous period**, 146 to 65 million years ago. Lizards are part of the animal group called **reptiles**, which is made up of several thousand different **species**.

Several characteristics make reptiles different from other animals. Reptiles are cold-blooded, or **ectothermic**. If the air gets too cold, then lizards slow down and eventually go into a deep sleep. A lizard's body temperature will change depending on its surroundings. Reptiles do not sweat, like humans, so they cool down by moving into a shaded area. To warm up they **bask** in the sunlight. Reptile skin is not elastic like human skin, but tougher and rougher, with no hair.

Introducing bearded dragons

Bearded dragons' native **habitat** is in central Australia. They are active during the day and spend their time in trees and basking on rocks in the woodlands and deserts. In hot weather "beardies" will burrow into the earth or hide under rocks. These lizards got their name from the spiked pouches around their throats that resemble beards. Bearded dragons may be brown, gray, or reddish-brown. They can change the shade of the color from light to dark to help regulate their body temperature.

Lizards love to bask in the sunshine. Sunlight helps them to produce vitamin D3 in their skin, which keeps them healthy.

YOUR RESPONSIBILITIES AS A PET OWNER

- ✪ Never buy a lizard without first discussing it with your family.

- ✪ Before getting a pet you must consider the bad as well as the good things involved in caring for the pet.

- ✪ Veterinary care for lizards can be very expensive. Your local **herpetological** society will offer advice. Before you get a lizard, find a vet who specializes in their care.

- ✪ Take an adult family member with you when you go to select your lizard.

- ✪ Never buy a pet because you feel sorry for it.

- ✪ Make sure the lizard you want was **bred** in **captivity**. Taking animals from the wild means that fewer lizards are able to rear young and keep their species alive. Animals bred in captivity are more likely to survive and flourish in captive conditions and should not have the **parasites** that are often found in reptiles caught in the wild.

Lizards under threat

Today, trail bikes and off-road vehicles are making tracks through the *beardies'* habitat. Those tracks wear the terrain down and allow erosion to occur. The land is also being dug up and completely changed by new housing developments. Currently the Australian government is working to protect specific areas for the bearded dragons and other animals. Groups are helping to educate people about the danger of habitat damage.

A lizard's eye has scales all around it, but no eyelashes.

Lizard Facts

Bearded dragons are one **species** of lizard that do make good pets, as long as they are well cared for. This book is based on bearded dragons, but the care advice applies to most other kinds of pet lizards, too. The **genus** to which bearded dragons belong is called *Pogona* and is comprised of many species, each with subtle differences. Two types of *Pogona* are *Pogona vitticeps*, the inland bearded dragon, and *Pogona barbata*, the coastal bearded dragon.

Starting out

It takes around two months for the eggs of the bearded dragon to hatch. The **hatchlings** feed on insects, spiders, and vegetation. As they grow, they shed their skin frequently. Throughout their lives, lizards spend time **basking** in the sun. They absorb full-spectrum **ultraviolet B (UVB)** light, which helps their bodies to produce vitamin D. With vitamin D, the bearded dragons can grow strong bones and muscles.

Pogona vitticeps (top) and *Pogona barbata* (bottom) originate in Australia and can be found across a wide expanse of territory.

Lizards as pets

Before purchasing a bearded dragon, you need to consider its typical daily behavior. Bearded dragons may be kept in a small group, but unless you intend to **breed** them, it would be better to have just one. If you plan to have more than one, remember that males will fight if kept together.

This bearded dragon is waving its arm to communicate.

When cage-mates are introduced, both lizards may start to wave their arms, as though greeting each other. This arm-waving, however, is simply a means of communicating with one another and assists in establishing **territorial** claims as well as dominance or submission.

IMPORTANT ADVICE

- ✪ Never put two male bearded dragons together.

- ✪ Never put two animals of different sizes together.

- ✪ Always have a veterinarian check a new pet before introducing it to one you already have.

Your pet may occasionally puff out and darken its throat (or beard). This happens in both male and female animals and shows that they are distressed or annoyed. Normally, when the beard darkens, the bearded dragon will bob its head up and down to make itself look more impressive.

The inland and coastal bearded dragons can both grow to a length of 25 centimeters (10 inches), from snout to vent (this means without the tail!). Females are smaller than males. Both species can live for about 10 years if well cared for, so owning a bearded dragon really is a long-term commitment.

Is a Lizard for You?

Before you purchase a bearded dragon, you must think very carefully. Is a bearded dragon the right pet for you? Are you the right person to own a bearded dragon? It can be very disappointing when you realize that the pet you wanted is not a realistic possibility, but it is better to understand this before you buy the pet and make it unhappy, too.

GOOD POINTS

✪ They can live for over seven years.

✪ They can be handled every few days.

✪ They can be purchased as babies and you can watch them grow.

✪ They only need to be fed once a day.

✪ They only need to be cleaned once a week (but spot cleaning should be done daily).

✪ They don't make any noise to disturb the neighbors.

✪ They become tame very easily.

Although they aren't soft and furry, lizards can be handled on a regular basis.

NOT-SO-GOOD POINTS

✪ Bearded dragons carry diseases that humans can catch (**zoonoses**) unless good hygiene precautions are taken.

✪ They require artificial heat to **maintain** their body temperature; this means that long walks outside are difficult, except on the very warmest of days.

✪ It can be very expensive to set up a bearded dragon's **vivarium**.

✪ It is sometimes difficult to provide the well-balanced, varied diet required to maintain a healthy bearded dragon. This will require time and effort from you.

✪ Veterinary treatment is expensive, and finding a vet experienced in treating **reptiles** can prove difficult. If your pet is sick, you may have to travel a long distance in order to find someone who can help.

✪ You will need to keep insects in your home, and there is a chance that some may escape!

Lizards like to eat lots of creepy-crawly live food. Is your family willing to have crickets in your house?

Some kinds of lizards, like this thorny devil lizard, are clearly very unsuitable to keep as pets!

Choosing a Bearded Dragon

It is very difficult to select a bearded dragon from a brief meeting at the pet store or breeder. You will have many questions that need answers. Most importantly, before you commit to purchasing your new companion, stand back and take a good look around the store. What do you see?

Take a good look at the lizards and the cage they are in at the pet store before you buy one.

THINGS YOU SHOULD SEE

- ✪ well-**ventilated** cages
- ✪ "guarded" heat sources that protect the animals inside from burning themselves
- ✪ thermostats controlling the heaters. This makes sure that the occupants don't get too hot or too cold!
- ✪ clean cages with fresh water
- ✪ **ultraviolet B (UVB)** lights should be fitted
- ✪ specimens should be bred in **captivity** with feeding records available
- ✪ insects on sale should be in good condition. Poor food will mean poor pets!

PROBLEMS TO WATCH OUT FOR

- ✪ mites or ticks
- ✪ dirty water bowls
- ✪ dirty cages
- ✪ lack of thermostats or UVB lights
- ✪ specimens caught in the wild.

One or two dragons?

It is perfectly acceptable to own one bearded dragon on its own. It will not feel "lonely" or "sad" as long as you make sure that it is in the correct environment.

Male or female?

If you do not plan to **breed** your pet, then it is best to keep a single male dragon. Females can have health problems if they are not allowed to breed and may need expensive veterinary care if they are unable to pass their eggs. Remember, many female lizards will lay eggs even if they do not have a mate. These eggs will not hatch.

Male and female bearded dragons look very similar, so make sure you check what sex your pet is before you buy it.

Buying your bearded dragon

The best place to buy your dragon is from a private breeder. If you have problems finding someone in your neighborhood, your local **herpetological** society should be able to help you. You should always take an adult with you when buying a pet.

These bearded dragons have just hatched. Young lizards are very delicate and should be handled very carefully.

What Do I Need?

A **vivarium** is a cage in which **reptile** owners house their pets. You can buy them at pet stores or make your own. They are normally made from glass or wood, and each type has its good points and its not-so-good points. In a vivarium you can control the warmth and **humidity** and make sure that live food cannot escape into your home. Never let a lizard run around your home unsupervised. It can get lost very quickly. Also, your lizard may be accidentally injured by curious family pets.

Glass vivariums

Glass vivariums can be bought from pet stores. They are easy to keep clean, which helps to prevent **infestations** of mites. However, they do not keep in warmth as easily as wooden vivariums, so it is important to make sure that the vivarium is always heated to the correct temperature for your lizard.

A glass vivarium can be a good home for a lizard. What other things are needed to make the lizard comfortable in its home?

You can make a vivarium

Use wood as the main construction material in the vivarium, except for the front of the cage, where sliding glass doors will give you easy access to the interior of the cage. The glass should be toughened and rounded at the edges to stop your lizard from hurting itself on rough areas. Wood will help the cage **maintain** the correct temperature. On the inside of the vivarium, all the places where the wood is joined together should be sealed with silicon rubber to help prevent both the leakage of water and an infestation of mites, which can **breed** rapidly in small gaps.

Shape and size

Ground-dwelling animals such as the bearded dragon prefer a vivarium that allows them room to investigate and move around, behaving as they would in the wild. A vivarium measuring 120 centimeters long, 60 centimeters deep, and 45 centimeters high (48 x 24 x 18 inches) should be adequate for a single lizard.

Ventilation

The amount of **ventilation** in the vivarium will depend on humidity requirements. Glass reptile vivariums from pet stores will come with built-in ventilation. If you make your own wooden vivarium then two vents, measuring about 5 centimeters by 8 centimeters (2 x 3 inches), are needed. One vent hole should be high on one side wall and the other should be lower on the opposite wall. Air circulation is improved by placing the vents at different levels. Each vent hole should be covered by a wire mesh that has very small holes, to prevent insects from escaping.

Proper ventilation is very important. It allows fresh air to enter the vivarium.

Heating

As an **ectothermic** reptile, your pet must have its body heat controlled artificially. You should create a warm area and a cool area in the cage. The warmest area, which your lizard will use for **basking**, should be 32 to 38 °Celsius (90 to 100 °Fahrenheit). Place the heaters toward one side of the vivarium, rather than in the middle. All heating units must be installed before putting the lizard in the vivarium. The heat these units provide must be measured with a thermometer and, if necessary, their position should be changed to ensure the correct temperature for your lizard. Heating supplies are easily available from pet stores and online supply companies. There are three main types:

❂ Ceramic heaters: They must be shielded.

❂ Spot bulbs: Various wattages are available. They must be shielded.

❂ Heat mats: These should cover less than one third of the cage-base; your lizard must be able to escape the heat if it wants to.

Safe basking areas are essential for your lizard's well-being. Notice that the heat source is shielded using a metal frame.

YOU WILL NEED:

- ✪ a thermostat to control heaters
- ✪ a securely fastened guard over all heat sources to protect your pet from burns
- ✪ wire mesh with small holes over vents to stop your lizard and insects from escaping
- ✪ thermometers to check for possible thermostat errors.

Check the humidity meter and thermometer regularly to ensure ideal conditions inside the vivarium.

Humidity

Humidity is the amount of water in the air. Low humidity can cause problems for reptiles when they are shedding their skin, as well as problems with their breathing. Different types of lizard need different levels of humidity. Humidity meters are available from pet stores and hardware stores and should be used to maintain levels around 35 percent for bearded dragons. Remember that ventilation will alter the level of humidity; an increase in ventilation will decrease humidity and vice versa.

WHAT HAPPENS IF THE HUMIDITY IS WRONG?

- ✪ respiratory problems (breathing difficulties)
- ✪ skin problems: blisters and infection
- ✪ eye infections
- ✪ infestation problems: mites, ticks, and flies.

Lighting

There are three main types of lighting used for reptiles:

✪ Full-spectrum **ultraviolet B (UVB)** light is very important for healthy bones and muscle control.

✪ Reflector bulbs (combined system) can be used with other heaters in larger cages.

✪ **Incandescent** bulbs can be used to create localized heat spots and are available in a variety of wattages. The bulb placement at one end of the vivarium depends on the amount of heat it produces. The proper placement must be figured out by using a thermometer before putting the lizard in the vivarium.

Ultraviolet light

UVB light helps many animals to produce vitamin D3 in their skin, which is then converted internally to the active vitamin D3. Without D3, reptiles are unable to absorb calcium. UVB lights should be left on for 10 to 14 hours daily and replaced every six months. There are several types of UVB lights available. Check with your local **herpetological** society.

Reflector bulbs

If reflector bulbs are used as a heat source, they can be used during the day along with a UVB bulb to give a daylight effect.

Bulbs will require changing periodically, so keep a spare one on hand.

If bulbs are used to create a "hot spot," then turn them off at night, as long as another heat source maintains the nighttime temperature between 24 and 27 °Celsius (75 and 80 °Fahrenheit). A wire guard should cover all reflector bulbs. A pattern of day and nighttime effects can reduce stress-related problems. Remember that your dragon will become distressed if it lives under white light for 24 hours a day, seven days a week. It is important to recreate the most natural conditions possible. In the wild, your lizard **species** would be used to a regular pattern of day and night.

You will need to move your lizard to a clean, temporary home *before* you start cleaning out the vivarium.

Hygiene

Food and water bowls should be removed, cleaned, and replaced daily. Do not place food and water bowls from the cage on surfaces in your kitchen, as this may spread disease. The vivarium should be regularly cleaned with a reptile-safe cleaner that can be bought at a pet store. Pay particular attention to corners, and dry the vivarium well before replacing your reptile. After handling animals and cleaning out the vivarium, make sure that you wash your hands with a mild disinfectant or antibacterial soap.

Everything must be removed from the vivarium and thoroughly cleaned. You must wear rubber gloves when cleaning the vivarium and its contents.

Substrate

Substrate is material placed at the bottom of the vivarium. Many products are available from pet stores, including bark (which maintains humidity), various sands, and reptile carpet. Some people use paper towels. You should remove any soiled substrate from the vivarium and renew it completely on a regular basis.

Bearded dragons love digging, so good-quality substrate is essential to keep them happy and healthy.

Lizards live well on calci-sand, which is sold in pet stores. Do not use sand containing silica, which has sharp edges and can injure a lizard. Some sands can cause your lizard to become **dehydrated** and die. Bags of children's play-sand are often sold as "silica-free" and are less expensive than other sands, but remember to check the label! Any substrate can cause problems if swallowed by your pet.

Plants

Real plants look attractive in the cage, but check that they are not poisonous to reptiles. Plastic plants often break into smaller pieces and can be easily swallowed, causing a blockage in the bowel. Information about safe plant species is constantly updated, and you should check this with your local herpetological society.

Green plants in the vivarium look nice, but they provide a place for insects to hide and will affect the humidity.

Cage furniture and hiding places

Furniture provides hiding places to help the lizard feel secure within the cage and reduce stress-related problems. Remember that it is your responsibility to help your new pet live a happy, relaxed life, so make sure it has plenty of hiding places.

Hiding places can be made from a variety of items such as plant pots, cardboard boxes with holes cut in the side, specially made caves, and anything hollow, even the inner section of a roll of toilet paper! A heavy rock that is completely stable and cannot be moved by your pet can also be placed in the vivarium. Make sure there aren't any sharp edges, as they can injure your animal.

Hatchling lizards will often go into a hiding place to find crickets that have hidden there. Hiding places provide a place for your reptile to feel safe. If your reptile feels unsafe, it will stop feeding. Hiding places should be placed in each of the warm, medium, and cool areas of your enclosure. Do not place the hiding places only in the coolest part of your cage, as a dragon will always choose security in the hiding place over warmth. It is best to place one hiding place in the middle of the cage, neither too close to nor too far from the heat source.

In the wild, lizards often hide between rocks and cracks to feel secure from **predators** and to escape from the heat of direct sunlight.

Caring for Your Lizard

There are several different foods that are suitable to feed to your bearded dragon. It is important to change your pet's food at different stages in its life. **Hatchling** dragons will eat a different diet from that of adults.

What to feed?

Your dragon is an omnivore. This means that it will eat both meat and vegetation. Examples of live food include fruit flies, mealworms, crickets, wax worms, small locusts, and garden insects. Make sure that the insects have been fed nutritious food before you feed them to your dragon. Place the insects in a secure container with fruit and vegetation for at least 24 hours before being fed to your pet. Well-fed insects will be a healthy meal for your lizard.

You may offer small mice, called pinkies, to adult lizards as a special treat. These are available frozen from pet stores.

TOP TIP

Never defrost **reptile** food in hot water. Place it in a sealed container in a cool area to thaw out slowly. A refrigerator is the best place to defrost your lizard's food items.

Remember to feed the insects fresh fruits and vegetables before you feed them to your lizard. Make sure you keep the box closed tightly!

Hatchlings

If you have purchased a hatchling dragon (from birth to three months of age), then offer it small crickets (around 1 centimeter, or 0.04 inch, long) three times a day. Offer as many crickets as your hatchling will eat before losing interest. These should be live to attract the hatchling's attention. Do not leave any uneaten insects in the cage. This is tempting on a busy day, but can result in an annoyed pet, as uneaten insects jump on and around your lizard. You can also feed your young pet finely cut green, leafy vegetables.

The greens you offer should be as varied as possible, but avoid dark greens such as spinach, as they upset the calcium levels in the dragon's body. Broad-leaf watercress and dandelion leaves are both suitable.

Salad should make up 20 percent of your dragon's diet.

TOP TIP

Do not feed mealworms to hatchling bearded dragons, as they are very hard to digest and may cause death.

Food can be used to tame your lizard. Always use tweezers when feeding your pet by hand in order to avoid accidental bites.

Juveniles

Once your lizard is four months old, feed it less often. Try offering medium-sized insects twice daily. If your pet shows little interest in the second feed, then offer food only once. Make sure that greens are offered every 48 hours, and never leave pieces of leaves in the enclosure for more than 12 hours. As your pet grows, the amount of greens it needs will increase to around 50 percent of its food.

Mealworms can be offered to your pet once it is over four months old. Use a variety of insects even if your lizard prefers one sort over another. Be careful with the size of food you offer your pet. As a general guide, the food must always be smaller than the space between your lizard's eyes.

TOP TIP

Always place greens in the coolest part of the cage.

Adults

Once your lizard is 18 months old, it is considered an adult. Adult dragons eat a wider variety of foods, including small mice, king worms, and mealworms. Adult dragons need to be fed every other day. Keep a close check on your pet, and if it starts to look thin, increase its meal. Record what food it is eating: remember that its survival depends on you.

Mealworms can be a tasty part of your bearded dragon's diet, and they are very nutritious, too.

Vitamin and mineral supplements

In **captivity**, lizards may not receive all the necessary elements of their diet. The most important mineral for bearded dragons is calcium carbonate, which is needed for healthy bones and muscles. This should be mixed into the greens as well as coated on any insects offered to your pet. If you fit a good quality **UVB** light to your cage, then no supplements will be needed apart from the pure calcium carbonate. Do not put any vitamins or minerals in drinking water, as it changes the taste and discourages your pet from drinking.

TOP TIPS

✪ Place a small amount of calcium powder in a plastic bag, put insects inside, and shake the bag gently until a coat of calcium covers the insects.

✪ Remove the water bowl and offer the insects to your dragon. Once your pet has finished eating, replace the water bowl and return any uneaten insects to their cage.

A plastic bag can be used to coat the insects with supplements.

Remember to place fresh water in the **vivarium** every day.

Treats

Wax worms are a tasty treat for a bearded dragon, though these should only be offered occasionally. Never offer cat food or dog food to a dragon, as this causes liver and kidney damage and can kill your pet.

Skin and nail care

When your lizard starts to shed its skin, spray a gentle mist of warm water over it to help the process along. Once it has shed, make sure that no pieces of skin are left on its toes or around its tail, as these could restrict its blood flow. If pieces of skin remain, occasional misting will help them drop off.

You can help your lizard file its own nails by including rocks with rough surfaces in the vivarium for it to crawl onto and scratch. The nails on your pet will need to be cut regularly so that they don't scratch you when you are handling it. You can use a pair of ordinary nail clippers, but be careful not to hurt your lizard or make its toes bleed. Ask a friend to hold it still, and only remove the very tip of the nail, usually less than 1 millimeter (0.04 inch). This will need to be done quite frequently.

Make sure that you never cut more than a millimeter off when trimming the lizard's nails.

Vacation care

It is never a good idea to leave your pet alone while you go away on vacation, even if it is just for the weekend. Always ask a responsible person to take care of your dragon. Pet stores and **herpetological** societies can suggest someone experienced in caring for bearded dragons.

CHECKING YOUR BEARDED DRAGON

It is very important that you check your pet regularly to make sure it is well.

Check that:

- ✪ your lizard has no mites or ticks on its body or in its cage
- ✪ there are no unusual lumps or swellings, particularly around its mouth
- ✪ no skin is stuck around its toes or tail
- ✪ its eyes are clear and bright and its nose is not blocked.

Taking your lizard to the vet

If your lizard gets sick, you will need to take it to the vet. Place your lizard in a container only slightly larger than itself. The box should be strong, have good **ventilation**, and be clearly marked with the words "This way up." Keep the box out of direct sunshine and drafts, and never leave it unattended. Lizards can die in hot motor vehicles, so plan your journey well and keep your pet with you at all times.

The box that your pet travels in should only be slightly larger than the lizard itself.

Can We Be Friends?

Reptiles are wild animals that have been **bred** in **captivity** for only a short period of time. They are not as friendly as dogs and cats. However, most bearded dragons bred in captivity are **hand-tamed** from a very early age and respond well to gentle handling for short periods of time. It will take time for your lizard to know your scent.

Be gentle and take your time!

When selecting your bearded dragon, make sure its eyes are bright and clean, it does not limp or have any signs of injury, and there are no sections of partially shed skin. Once you are at home, let your pet become accustomed to its **vivarium**. For the first week you will only be able to watch your lizard and feed it. It is tempting to pick it up and show it to your family and friends, but it must have time to get used to its new cage.

Let your lizard get used to you slowly. Just watching it instead of picking it up will also help you to understand your new friend's habits much better!

After the first week of patiently feeding and caring for your new dragon comes the time to handle it for a few minutes. Gently lift it out of the cage in a warm room and sit on the floor with it on your hand. Make sure you are in a room where it can easily be caught if it runs away! Time how long you have it out of the cage; remember that it depends on its cage to keep its body warm. After ten minutes put it back gently and offer it some food. Never handle it immediately after feeding or you may make it **regurgitate** its food.

HOW TO PICK UP YOUR LIZARD

Pick up your lizard by placing one hand under its stomach and then, supporting its full weight in the palm of your hand, scoop it up. Remember not to make any sharp, jerky movements, as this will make it think that you could be a **predator**. Never pick a lizard up by its tail, as this can cause it damage!

Always support your lizard's body when you handle it.

Meeting other lizards

It is not a good idea to introduce your bearded dragon to other lizards. Unlike **mammals**, bearded dragons do not feel the need for sharing or company; they will not feel sad if they are housed alone for their entire lives. If you still want to get another lizard, make sure that they are female and of a similar size. Two males will probably fight. The new bearded dragon should be housed separately until you are certain it is healthy. If the two lizards do not get along, you will need to set up another vivarium and keep your pets separate.

Be very careful when you introduce your lizard to another lizard. They are not used to having much company.

Never let your pet meet other animals such as dogs and cats. Dogs and cats are predators of lizards and may injure or kill them. No matter what type of vivarium you are using, it is important to make sure that all access panels, whether they are from the top or the front, are securely locked.

Always keep the vivarium shut securely, especially if you have other animals in the house.

Harnesses and collars

Many types of harness are available from pet stores. If you find a suitable lizard harness, it will allow you to take your pet outside during warm, sunny days. Make sure there are no predators around. Natural sunlight is better than all of the artificial **UVB** lights in pet stores, and this will be very healthy for your pet.

Taking your lizard for a walk can be fun for you and your pet.

Keep your distance when you feed your lizard.

Biting

It is very rare for bearded dragons bred in captivity to bite their owners. If this happens it is probably an accident at feeding time. Remember not to feed your pet with your fingers. Place food items in a pair of tweezers and hold them close to your lizard. If you are bitten, dragons will often let go right away. If they don't, then try not to pull your hand away, as this will cause more damage to your skin. Be patient and it will let go after a short while. Make sure that you use a mild disinfectant on the bitten area once the lizard has been removed. If the bite has broken your skin, you should visit your doctor.

Fun Time Together

Bearded dragons do not play in the same way as other pets. They won't fetch a stick as a dog might, and they are very slow to learn new tricks! Some animal behaviorists believe that you can train lizards, but in reality it is very hard to know when your bearded dragon is having fun.

It is important to give it a good-quality cage and to change the layout of its environment once every few weeks. Have a selection of different hiding places and rocks. After cleaning the **vivarium**, change the position of the rocks, making sure that you have a hiding place in the middle of the enclosure and at each end to prevent a feeling of insecurity. Empty cardboard boxes and cartons will be of great interest to your pet and serve a useful purpose in keeping it stimulated by its environment.

It is very tempting to take your pet out of the cage for long periods of time. You can take your pet out once a day at the very most. It won't forget you or suddenly become unfriendly.

The arrangement in the vivarium can be changed occasionally to provide stimulation for your pet.

Does my bearded dragon like to be handled?

It can be very hard to know if your pet is happy to have you pick it up and cuddle it. Watch its behavior. If it is bobbing its head or its beard turns a darker color, then put it back in its cage. Reward your lizard when it goes back to its vivarium with a favorite snack. But remember that it is more likely that lizards put up with being handled rather than actually enjoying it.

You can put *boxes* and *paper towel rolls* in the vivarium as a new hiding place for your lizard.

You can *keep a track of your lizard's behavior* and how long you handled it by making a note of the behavior and time on a chart.

Keeping Your Lizard Healthy

Before buying your lizard, ask a few vets if they specialize in **reptiles**. Usually vets can handle pet emergencies, but many do not specialize in reptile care. You must think about veterinary care because it is expensive and there may not be a reptile vet near your home.

There are no special **vaccinations** necessary for either you or your lizard, but it is advisable to let your doctor know that you own reptiles, and make sure that your **tetanus** vaccination is up-to-date.

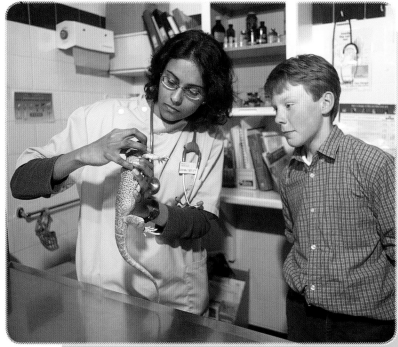

If your lizard is sick you must take it to the veterinarian, who will examine it and prescribe the relevant treatment.

If you have a male bearded dragon, there will be no need to have it **neutered**. If you have bought a female and don't intend to **breed** from her, then this may need to be done later in life if she has problems laying her eggs. It may be difficult to tell the sex of your new pet if it is a **hatchling**. Don't worry—most single animals will be perfectly healthy without neutering. However, it is worth making sure that you know what to do and whom to contact in the event of an emergency.

Can I prevent common diseases?

Most health problems in lizards are caused by poor care and poor cage maintenance. Over 90 percent of reptile diseases do not occur in the wild, only in animals in **captivity**. This shows how important it is to give your lizard good food and an appropriate **vivarium**, and to change its **UVB** light source every six months. Make sure the temperature in the cage is correct and that there is an area where it can cool down.

This lizard looks alert and healthy. You must observe your pet every day for any signs of illness. Early diagnosis means early recovery.

Treatment of lizards for **parasites** can be given by mouth.

ZOONOSES

When you care for your lizard, be careful about keeping yourself healthy, too. **Zoonoses** are diseases that may be transferred from animals to humans. The best-known reptile zoonosis is infection by the bacteria *Salmonella*. People can become infected with *Salmonella* from reptiles. To avoid this, follow some simple rules:

- ✪ Wash your hands with an antibacterial handwash after handling any reptile, cage, or accessory.

- ✪ Wear gloves when cleaning the vivarium and all of its contents.

- ✪ Disinfect cages regularly.

- ✪ Keep young children away from reptiles. Older children should always be supervised.

- ✪ Keep reptiles and their equipment away from food preparation areas.

- ✪ Clean bites or scratches immediately with an antibacterial cream. If the bite has broken the skin or the scratch is deep, see a doctor.

Always wear rubber gloves when you clean the vivarium. Make sure you don't miss the edges and corners of the cage, as bacteria can hide there.

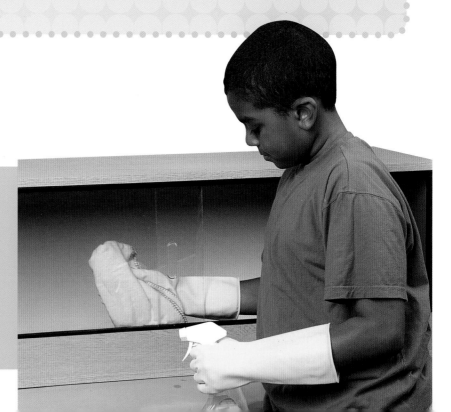

If your lizard bites you, ask an adult to help you disinfect the wound using antibacterial cream. If the wound is deep, you must go to the doctor.

A darkened beard means a dragon is under stress. When this happens, it is best to leave your lizard alone in a quiet room in its cage.

Some Health Problems

Poor diet or environmental conditions cause most diseases commonly seen in **reptiles** in **captivity**. Many of the problems with pet lizards are simply not found in lizards from the wild. The more a lizard feels at home in a well-planned cage, the healthier your animal will be.

Abscesses

Any wound that becomes infected can develop into an **abscess**. Common causes include poor hygiene, overcrowding, and stress. If **territorial** animals, such as two males, are kept together with not enough space to form separate territories, one will attack the other. An injury from an attack may develop into an abscess. Treatment involves surgical removal of the abscess and making sure that whatever caused it is fixed.

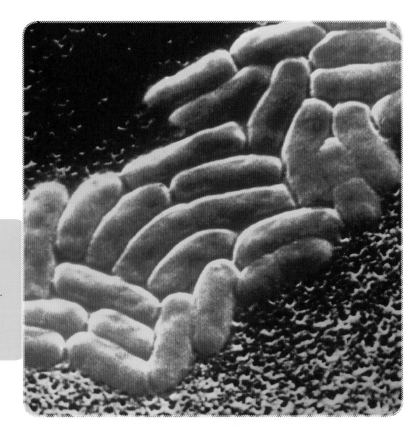

Infection of wounds by bacterial colonies like these can cause abscesses to form.

Metabolic bone disease

In metabolic bone disease, bones become low in calcium and break easily. Lizards who have it may suffer from fractured limbs, a swollen lower jaw, weakness in the limbs (a healthy lizard should be able to lift its body clear of the ground), loss of appetite, and in the later stages, collapse, muscle tremors, and breathing problems. The causes are often linked to poor care of the animal, with lack of **UVB** light and poor diet being the main reasons.

If a lizard is badly affected, weekly calcium injections may be required. Some lizards can have a moderate to severe form of the disease, although their owners may be unaware that there is a problem.

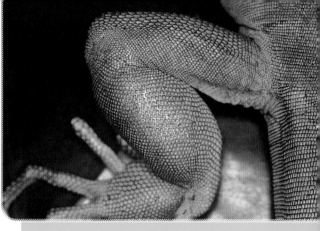

Swollen legs like this one are often a sign that your lizard may have metabolic bone disease.

This lizard has a visibly diseased jaw. This is another symptom of metabolic bone disease.

Respiratory disease

Signs of respiratory disease include a runny nose, sneezing, wheezing, labored breathing, and open-mouthed breathing. A simple infection of the nose can easily become pneumonia if untreated. The most common cause is **bacterial** infection, although **viruses**, **fungi**, and **parasites** can also be involved. Very sick animals require hospitalization for intensive treatment such as fluid therapy and force-feeding. Milder infections may respond to antibiotics alone.

Many antibiotics are made for **mammals** or other warm-blooded animals, so if you don't increase the cage temperature, the antibiotics may not work. Some viral and bacterial infections may be transmitted from you to your pet and so, if you are unwell, ask a member of your family or a friend to take care of your pet for a few days to reduce the risk of cross-infection. Always keep your pet and its **vivarium** clean to reduce the risk of an infection occurring.

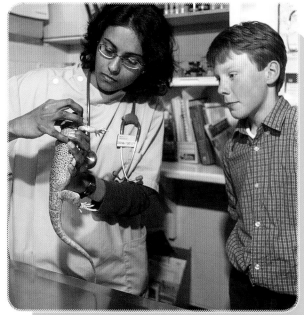

Internal parasites

A parasite is an **organism** that depends completely on another organism for its food and nourishment and to complete its life cycle. All reptiles caught in the wild are likely to have internal parasites. A sample of **feces** must be tested in order

The vet uses a syringe to give the lizard a dose of antibiotics.

to tell if the reptile has parasites. Parasites slow animals' growth rates and make them more likely to catch diseases. The vet may recommend that your adult lizard gets a worm treatment at least once a year. If left untreated, parasites can cause death.

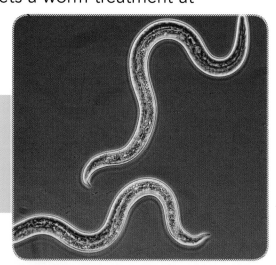

Nematode worms like these often infect lizards and can have very harmful effects on their health.

Worming is carried out by a vet either putting a solution inside the lizard's mouth or by a small injection. This is often repeated after 10 to 14 days. Lizards with parasites may have different symptoms, such as diarrhea or worms moving around in their feces.

External parasites

Parasites that live on the outside of your lizard are called external parasites. Mites and ticks are commonly found and spread very quickly. These are blood-sucking parasites that, in large numbers, may cause **anemia**. They may also contribute to the spread of other diseases between reptiles. These parasites enter the cage on your pet or on a piece of equipment that you have just purchased from a place where there is an active **infestation**. None of these parasites should be left untreated.

Ticks are relatively large so they are easy to spot, although they may hide in big body cavities such as the nostrils. Individual ticks may be removed with tweezers, but be careful not to leave the mouthparts behind in the reptile's skin—this can lead to the formation of abscesses. It is better to get a vet to do this for you, though many experienced reptile owners will have carried out this procedure and may offer to help you.

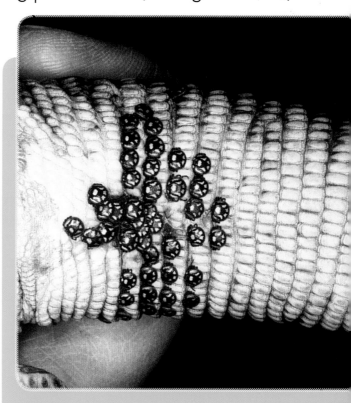
This lizard has an infestation of ticks on its tail.

Mites

Mites are smaller than ticks and are able to hide under single scales. They are often present in large numbers and thrive on sick animals. Mites may be noticed crawling on the owner's skin

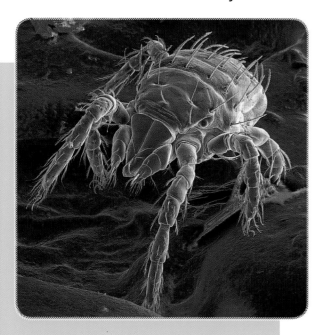

immediately after handling the reptile or floating dead in the water bowl. The mites do not generally bite people. A single female mite can lay up to 100 eggs in tiny spaces in the cage. This means that treating the cage in addition to the animal is very important. The vet will give your lizard the appropriate treatment for mite infestations. Some treatments are not 100 percent safe for both reptiles and their owners.

This picture of a mite has been magnified hundreds of times. Mites are relatives of spiders and have eight legs.

TREATMENTS TO GET RID OF MITES

Always ask the advice of your vet about suitable parasite treatments if you think that your lizard has mites.

The vet can treat your lizard for mites and help it return to good health.

Tail shedding

Tail shedding is a way that many **species** of lizard escape **predators** in the wild. If a predator grasps the tail, it will drop off and often twitch to distract the predator's attention. This shedding of the tail does not harm the lizard, but it does cause some distress. Do not grab or pull your lizard's tail. If a lizard does shed its tail, eventually the tail will grow back, although it will not look identical to the original one! The old tail can be disposed of.

Tail shedding is a distress signal. Never hold your lizard by the tail, as this may cause the lizard to shed it!

Keeping a Record

To help decide whether your pet is growing healthily and developing well, it is important to keep accurate records on your computer or in a notebook. Over time it is difficult to remember whether your lizard fed or went to the bathroom on certain days in the past few weeks, let alone months.

Make a note of whether or not your pet has been eating. Remember that if it doesn't eat for a few days or more you may need to take it to the vet to be checked over. There may be a reason why it has lost its appetite or that feeding has become difficult. It is very important to notice whether or not your pet lizard is going to the bathroom. Blockages of the bowel are very common, and life-saving treatment or surgery depends on you noticing quickly that there is a problem and contacting the vet.

You can make a colorful scrapbook about your pet using photos, drawings, and notes about your time spent together.

Records can help to tell you if you may need to take your lizard to see the vet, and copies of any notes should be taken with you if you decide to go to the veterinary clinic. This information will help the vet figure out the problem your pet is having and possibly recommend other ways to care for your lizard.

Why not put photographs of the two of you together at different stages in your lizard's life to make a scrapbook? You can take this to school and show your friends all about your pet and how you care for it.

Remember to get your family to take photos of you with your lizard.

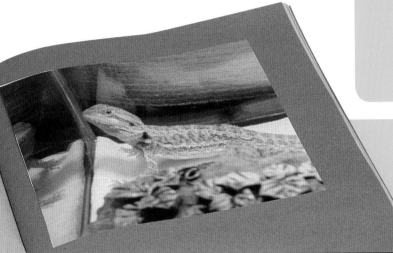

Keeping a detailed record sheet will help you **maintain** up-to-date information about your pet's health.

RECORD SHEET

Species . . . .
Sex . . . .   Age . . . .
Diet . . . .
Frequency . . . .
Temperature (day) . . . . (night) . . . .
UVB light period—12 hours per day

Date	Weight	Appetite	Thirst	Urine	Feces	What we did today	Caregiver

When a Lizard Dies

If you provide your bearded dragon with the best enclosure you are able to, re-create its natural **habitat** to the best of your ability, and give it a good diet, it should live for a good number of years. Bearded dragons should live for about 7 to 10 years and, as knowledge about them and equipment for keeping them in **captivity** improves, they are likely to live longer.

But no matter how well you care for your pet, one day it will die. Perhaps it will die peacefully in its sleep, or you, your parents, and your vet might need to make a decision together in order to prevent your lizard from suffering unnecessarily. It is never easy to decide when is the "right" time to have your lizard **put down** by the vet. Part of you will always want just one extra day to take your pet home and say goodbye privately. If your lizard is in pain, then as a true friend you will need to be strong and allow the vet to end the suffering.

As your lizard gets older, it may spend more time resting.

Feeling upset

Whether your pet passes away in its sleep or at the vet's, you will feel upset. It is perfectly natural to cry when you think of your pet leaving your life. You will have become very attached to your pet and will miss it. But after a period of time the pain will become less and you will remember the happy times you spent together.

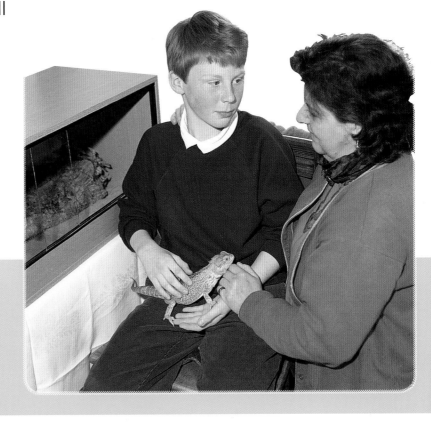

If your lizard becomes too weak due to illness or old age, you may have to make the difficult decision of having it put down.

You can make a burial mound to mark your lizard's grave.

Glossary

abscess soft lump filled with pus

anemia illness where there are not enough red blood cells in the blood, making the animal weak

bacterial caused by bacteria

bask lie exposed to warmth or sunlight

breed keep animals and encourage them to mate so they produce young

captivity under the control of humans; not in the wild

Cretaceous period time in history when flowering plants first appeared and dinosaurs lived

dehydrated dried out, or losing water in the body enough to cause discomfort or illness

ectothermic dependent on external sources to keep body warm (cold-blooded)

feces solid waste matter passed out of the body

fungi types of living things that get food by absorbing other living or decaying material

genus grouping term used to classify animals or plants

habitat place where an animal or plant lives or grows

hand-tame raised by humans with lots of time spent in training

hatchling recently hatched infant

herpetological to do with the study of reptiles and amphibians

humidity moisture in the air

incandescent emitting light as a result of being heated

infestation presence (of parasites) in large numbers, often causing damage or disease

maintain keep at the same level or rate, keeping in good condition by checking on something regularly

mammal animal with fur or hair on its body that feeds its babies with milk

neuter perform an operation that stops lizards from having babies

organism living thing

parasite small creature, such as a tick or worm, that lives on or in another animal's body and usually harms them

predator animal that hunts and kills other animals for food

put down give a sick animal an injection to help it die peacefully and without pain.

regurgitate bring swallowed food up again to the mouth

reptile cold-blooded animal with scaly or rough skin

Salmonella kind of bacteria

species kind or particular sort of living creature

substrate soft material to put in the bottom of a lizard cage

territorial defending an area of space that an animal sees at its own

tetanus disease caused by bacteria

ultraviolet B (UVB) invisible (to humans) part of light that produces vitamin D3 in lizards' skin

vaccination injection that is given to protect against a disease

ventilation air that enters and circulates freely in a closed space

virus type of microorganism that causes illness

vivarium cage for amphibians or reptiles

zoonosis (plural: **zoonoses**) any disease that can be transmitted to humans from animals

Find Out More

Books

Au, Manfred. *Bearded Dragons*. Hauppauge, N.Y.: Barron's, 2009.

Bartlett, Richard D., and Patricia Pope Bartlett. *Bearded Dragons*. Hauppauge, N.Y.: Barron's, 2009.

Bartlett, Richard D., and Patricia Pope Bartlett. *Lizard Care from A to Z*. Hauppauge, N.Y.: Barron's, 2009.

Purser, Philip. *Bearded Dragons*. Neptune City, N.J.: T. F. H., 2006.

Websites

www.beardeddragon.org
This website has lots of information, photos, and advice about how to care for your pet, written by other bearded dragon owners.

www.beardeddragoncare.net
This website has lots of information about feeding, handling, and providing the right habitat for your bearded dragon.

http://nationalzoo.si.edu/Animals/ReptilesAmphibians/Facts/Fact-Sheets/Inlandbeardeddragon.cfm
This website of the Smithsonian National Zoological Park has information about the bearded dragon, as well as other reptiles.

Index